Original title:
Philosophical Thoughts from My Bed

Copyright © 2025 Creative Arts Management OÜ
All rights reserved.

Author: Jameson Hartfield
ISBN HARDBACK: 978-1-80566-037-8
ISBN PAPERBACK: 978-1-80566-332-4

The Courage to Question from Under the Duvet

Beneath my blanket fortress, I ponder the skies,
What if socks have feelings? What if they lie?
The world is absurd, like a cat in a hat,
Sometimes I just wish it would all fall flat.

Driftwood of the Mind in a Sea of Sheets

My thoughts float like driftwood on waves of my dreams,

>A pillow the captain, or so it seems.
>I navigate whims on this quilted boat,
>Wishing for wisdom to keep me afloat.

Sacred Stillness and the Art of Reflection

In the stillness of morning, reflections appear,
Like toast in the toaster, my thoughts reappear.
Is existence just bread, or perhaps it's the jam?
If life's a great sandwich, I'm the confused ham.

Comfort's Embrace and the Nature of Existence

Wrapped in my duvet, I seek answers bold,
Are we merely stories that history told?
With crumbs of breakfast and dreams left unspent,
I laugh at my questions, they're all well-intent.

The Mind's Lullaby

As I lay here, dreams take flight,
Minds play tricks in soft twilight.
Are my socks missing? A grand heist done?
Or just my brain playing hide and run?

Thoughts like clouds, they form and part,
Wisdom whispers, 'Don't lose heart.'
Is my pillow smarter than my head?
It knows my secrets, all unsaid.

Fables of the Slumbering Soul

Once a blanket named Maurice,
Told tales of the universe, oh so fierce.
Did it matter if cheese fell down?
The stars just giggled, lost in crown.

Pajamas danced like joyful sprites,
While I pondered my late-night bites.
Is ice cream a food or a dream?
In a sleepy state, it's both, it seems.

Ponderings at Dawn's Threshold

Morning light creeps, what do I see?
The cat plotting world domination, quite free.
Do socks have feelings, or so I muse?
Their lonely lives, do they choose to snooze?

Breakfast debates, toast or cereal?
The scale whispers truth, how imperial.
Should I rise or linger in this shell?
A lazy dance, who knows me well?

The Pillow's Silent Wisdom

In quietude, my pillow knows,
Of dreams where my laundry magically goes.
Will tomorrow bring chores or a snack?
The wisdom here? Don't cut me slack!

The moon's a witness to my plight,
As I argue with pajamas at night.
Do my dreams wear capes or just despair?
Either way, they're floating in air.

Gazing at the Universe Through a Window of Thought

Stars above me twinkle bright,
Wondering who's wrong or right.
Do aliens laugh at our plight,
Or just wave from their satellite?

Is life a joke, or is it grand?
Do squirrels plot while we just stand?
Are we the punchline in their band?
I'd ask, but I can't understand.

Carpeted Reflections on Life's Path

On this rug, I sit and muse,
Decisions made, which way to choose?
Should I soar high or snooze?
With all that pondering, I'll likely lose!

I once dreamt of a life so wise,
But reality wore a comic disguise.
Was that a fortune cookie prize?
Or just my mom showing me the lies?

Seeking Answers in the Softness of Night

Under blankets, thoughts take flight,
Do pillows judge my wit tonight?
If dreams are true, all feels right,
But in the morning, it's back to sight.

I question if my cat can see,
The weight of life, what's it to me?
Paws on my chest, his purr is key,
We both agree—just let it be.

Meditations Wrapped in Cotton and Dreams

Wrapped in sheets that feel like air,
I ponder deep, do penguins care?
They waddle through, so debonair,
While I'm here, pondering a s'more affair.

Cotton clouds in my sleepy head,
Are they more alive than the living dead?
With each thought, I'm wildly led,
What's for breakfast? This could be spread!

The Mind's Escape from Daylight

In the sheets, my thoughts take flight,
A pillow's dive, into the night.
Is this wisdom or just dread?
Perhaps I should just stay in bed.

The sun's a bully, bright and bold,
Stealing dreams I dare not hold.
What are chores but mockery's call?
Fine, I'll rise, but I'll not enthrall.

Imagining the Infinite in Four Walls

Four walls hug me like a friend,
Crafting thoughts that twist and bend.
What if life's a cozy nook?
A plot twist in a silly book?

Outside, they race in frantic glee,
While I sip tea and watch TV.
Perhaps, I'm wise to simply sway,
In comfy robes, I'll greet the day.

Bathed in Starlight, Bound by Thought

Beneath a blanket, stars collide,
Mind's eye travels far and wide.
Do aliens ponder from their beds?
Or do they just eat cosmic spreads?

Every twinkle sparks a joke,
As I munch my midnight croak.
Crickets chirp a lullaby tune,
While I argue with the moon.

The Philosophical Quilt of Life's Mosaic

Life's a quilt of patches bright,
Stitched from laughter, sewn with plight.
What if each thread holds a dream?
And bedbugs share the cosmic scheme?

I ponder deep, yet chuckle loud,
As thoughts parade, a silly crowd.
In the fabric, wisdom lies,
But I just nap, much to my surprise.

Fleeting Thoughts Under a Cloudy Sky

Beneath gray fluff, I ponder wide,
Comfy blankets become my guide.
Is a cloud just a thought in a rush?
Or a dream that forgot how to blush?

Cereal fills my mind with cheer,
As I contemplate the day that's near.
Socks mismatched, in a colorful flare,
Who needs a reason? Just sit and stare.

The Chamber of Unvoiced Ideas

In a room where silence reigns,
Whispers linger like sweet refrains.
A toothbrush debates with a lonely sock,
While daydreams dance with the ticking clock.

The pillow plots world domination,
With its fluff and cushy sensation.
Could the remote control win a prize?
Or is the cat the biggest surprise?

Comfort's Cradle and the Weight of Wonder

Within this space where thoughts collide,
A donut-shaped void, I can't abide.
What if goldfish held secret plans?
Or the dust bunnies formed tiny clans?

Each zzz I take, a venture grand,
Exploring realms where I make the stand.
But breakfast calls, a hero's quest,
To conquer cereal, I must invest.

Catching Fireflies of Imagination Indoors

With a net of dreams, I sweep the floor,
Hoping to catch thoughts galore.
Bouncing light against the wall,
Each flicker begs me to enthrall.

Mismatched chairs hold witty debates,
About the fate of socks and plates.
What happens when the toast gets burnt?
Do we cry, or do we learn?

A Dreamer's Dialogue with the Stars

Oh stars, you twinkle, what do you know?
Do you whisper secrets to planets down below?
Chasing comets, I ponder the night,
Do they laugh at our cosmic plight?

From my bed, I'm an astronaut bold,
Navigating dreams like treasures untold.
With every snore I launch my quest,
Are wishes just thoughts in a cosmic jest?

Starlit Queries in the Bedroom

What is reality? A myth in disguise?
Do my socks on the floor hold the key to the skies?
While I'm trapped here beneath this quilt,
Is the universe laughing, or is it just guilt?

A light so bright, yet my mind feels dim,
Do I wish on stars or just hope my dreams swim?
Pajamas snug, I question it all,
Is there logic behind a night owl's call?

Pillow Forts and Existential Questions

In my pillow fort, I'm a wise sage,
Contemplating life like I'm on a stage.
If my blanket could speak, what tales would it spin?
Do dreams take a break when I'm ready to win?

I sip my cocoa, a philosopher brave,
Is the cookie just sweet, or is it my save?
With crumbs on my chin, I ponder away,
Is snack time the key to a brighter day?

The Stillness That Sparks Inquiry

In silence so loud, I hear my brain's hum,
Is that wisdom I seek, or just the last crumb?
Thoughts float like dust in the moon's soft beam,
Are we all just players in one endless dream?

With a sigh, I stretch, feeling cosmic delight,
Does the universe notice my silly plight?
Maybe I'm stargazing while lying in bed,
Creating worlds woven from nonsense instead.

Awakening Thoughts in the Land of Nod

In dreams where socks do dance and twirl,
I ponder why my pillows whirl.
Why is cheese so great at two?
And why do llamas wear a shoe?

Do sheep count humans just for fun?
Or do they hide from the morning sun?
With blankets wrapped like cozy hugs,
I chase my thoughts like playful bugs.

The Simple Wisdom of Cozy Hours

What if my cat runs the universe?
Does she know I'm her loyal verse?
If worlds can spin on a cozy bed,
Surely, I can too, with thoughts in my head.

Is toast a meal, or just a slice?
Do pickles ever think they're nice?
As I cradle dreams of cheese and pie,
The universe answers with a sigh.

A Symphony of Delicate Queries

In the realm of quilts and thoughts so bright,
I wonder if a dream takes flight.
What if socks could start a band?
Would they rock or take a stand?

Do chairs ever wish to join the dance?
Or do they only dream of chance?
With snuggles deep and laughter near,
My mind's a stage for thoughts sincere.

Tracing Ideas on the Canvas of Night

If I scribble dreams on my pillow's face,
Do they hold a secret, a hidden place?
Does my bed know all my schemes?
Or just giggle at my silly dreams?

Will breakfast ever learn its role?
Or is it scrambled, like a soul?
Each thought a tickle, a playful jest,
In this cozy nook, I find my rest.

The Stillness of Seeking

Lying here in cozy bliss,
I ponder life's great essence.
What if socks have feelings too?
Would they be in a sock sense?

The blanket folds like time's own map,
Adventure waits in slumber's grip.
Exploring realms with no shoe tap,
I might just take an epic trip.

Beneath the sheets, the world feels wide,
Imagined views from this small port.
The popcorn ceiling, a starry guide,
Craving wisdom from home court.

A Restful Mind's Odyssey

With pillows stacked like mountains high,
I sail across my quilted sea.
Cereal bowls and crumby pie,
A feast for thought, oh, just for me.

The clock ticks on, its hand a tease,
It laughs as I drift, reclined and free.
Each tick a wave, a gentle breeze,
To ponder all, yet let it be.

What if my cat teaches me grace?
Or the spider spins tales of old?
Insomnia is a funny race,
No prize for wisdom, just a fold.

Whispers of Midnight Contemplation

The moon peeks in, a silver grin,
As I debate the snack I'll nab.
In this cozy realm, where dreams begin,
Should I have chips or a savory slab?

Pondering the laws of socks and shoes,
Can they coexist without a fight?
What if they form their own little crews,
Having parties far into the night?

The whispers here, they tickle my ear,
They say that toast can cure the gloom.
But what of the crumbs that disappear?
A cereal mystery in my room.

Dreams Wrapped in Solitude's Embrace

Tangled sheets, a cozy nest,
In solitude, I float and sway.
What if dreams put me to the test?
But I'd rather snack and drift away.

The world outside can spin and race,
While I lounge in this quiet space.
Debates with pillows, a friendly face,
All wrapped in a sleepy embrace.

Oh, the wonders that I create,
In this kingdom of fluff and thread.
I reign supreme—it feels so great,
As I drift through thoughts, half-asleep in bed.

Reflections Beneath the Covers

Laying here in woolen bliss,
Dreams and snacks, what's not to miss?
Thoughts of laundry, chores galore,
But my bed whispers, "Just one more!"

Should I rise, or stay a while?
Outside, the sun does beckon, smile.
Yet here I dwell, a cozy sea,
Where even time can't bother me.

Questions Piled High on Fluffy Pillows

Why does cereal sink in milk?
And who knit this blanket of silk?
If cats could talk, what would they say?
"More treats, please!" or, "Let's nap all day!"

Is breakfast better served in bed?
Or should I rise and use my head?
A swirling mess of thoughts today,
While pillow forts come out to play.

The Mind's Lantern Glows at Dawn

Morning light creeps through my blinds,
Unruly thoughts, like tangled twines.
Does coffee count as a solid meal?
Or just a potion to help me feel?

Dreams of grandeur fade with haste,
As I ponder on noodle-based fate.
Should I conquer the world today?
Or simply explore my sandwich array?

Sleep's Soft Debate with Consciousness

Is it sleep or is it bliss?
Logic fades, but joy I kiss.
Debating deep, I doze and dream,
While reasoning's just a muted gleam.

Who needs a plan when cozy reigns?
Each second's bliss softens all pains.
In this haven I redefine,
Life's absurdities, wrapped in twine.

Whispers in the Night

Under the covers, I ponder life,
Does my cat dream of fish or strife?
The curtains rustle, a breeze takes flight,
I giggle at shadows that dance with delight.

Should I be deep in sleep's warm embrace,
Or scroll through my phone at a feverish pace?
The clock ticks loudly, a pulse in the dark,
Is this what they mean by 'finding your spark'?

Thoughts of cereal at three not so tame,
Is breakfast really the best meal or a game?
I laugh at the moon, it's laughing too,
In this dance of thoughts, what else can I do?

Then whispers emerge, a soft silent tease,
Are they bringing answers, or just here to tease?
I settle back down, this bed is a throne,
Where musings unravel, I'm never alone.

Contemplations Beneath the Sheets

Beneath the blankets, I question the stars,
Are they distant dreams or just cosmic cars?
If I were a comet, would I leave a trail,
Or get lost in the clutter, like socks without a pair?

The pillow agrees, quite odd, I'd say,
Why do we worry about tomorrow's gray?
A sandwich I left, forgotten and sleek,
Is it a snack or a lesson? Oh brain, don't peek!

My teddy holds secrets of whims and of fears,
In this cozy nook, I've confided for years.
Is the universe listening? My heart has a shout,
Does it think I'm profound, or just a bit stout?

With dreams as my guides, I toss and I turn,
Is wisdom just laughter? Oh how will I learn?
Soon the dawn rises, like a show on a stage,
My blanket retreats, but oh what a wage!

Dreams of a Sleepwalker

As I drift off, my mind starts to roam,
Am I best friends with a llama named Jerome?
He says life's a circus, with clowns all around,
In sleepwalking realms, reality's drowned.

The fridge becomes mountains, so tall and so grand,
I trek through my kitchen, a magical land.
Where jellybeans rain down, and music plays loud,
In slippers, I conquer, I'm feeling quite proud.

But what if I'm trapped in my own snooze-fest?
What if tomorrow's just a quest for some rest?
I giggle and wiggle with newfound delight,
For who knows my fate, when I leap from the height?

With tales yet untold, I dash in my dreams,
A hero of nonsense, or so it would seem.
I wake with a grin, and a sigh, what a flair,
Here's to sleepwalking, and finding my chair!

Reflections in a Duvet

In the cocoon of cotton, the world feels so near,
Are socks the lost friends we hide from in fear?
With each flip of the sheets, I muse in delight,
What's life without laughter in dead of the night?

A cup of hot cocoa, or two, maybe three,
Is the sweetness a gift or a curse? Let me see.
Each sip is a whisper, a wise, soothing friend,
Plans for tomorrow? Just let the night bend.

Wondering if pillows have secrets to share,
Do they laugh at our dreams with a feathery glare?
As I chuckle and cringe at each curious thought,
Who knew bed-bound musings could stir a good plot?

So here's to reflections, both silly and bright,
In my duvet adventure, the world seems just right.
With laughter as my guide in this cozy embrace,
I'll dance in my dreams at this sweet, safe pace.

A Sanctuary of Solitude

In the cocoon of blankets tight,
I ponder life, with snacks in sight.
The world outside, so loud and bright,
Yet here, my thoughts take playful flight.

A cat's soft purr, my trusted guide,
In this stillness, I confide.
Why rush to meet the daily tide?
When here, I can just enjoy the ride.

The ceiling fan spins tales untold,
Of ancient wisdom, and tales of old.
With popcorn dreams, both sweet and bold,
In this quiet, life's truths unfold.

So let the world turn, fast or slow,
I'll brew my musings, watch them grow.
In the haven of my cozy throw,
I find the joy in all I know.

Musings in the Dark

In shadows deep, I sit and grin,
Contemplating where to begin.
What's the purpose, where's the spin?
Is life a race, or just a whim?

With a slice of cake on my knee,
I question fate and destiny.
Does choice matter, or is it free?
Will my next snack be green tea, maybe?

The light from the fridge starts to glow,
A sign that it's time for a show.
Should I ponder or just let go?
A balance lies in yes and no.

So here in dark, I play and tease,
With thoughts like bubbles, floating free.
Amidst the giggles, I find my ease,
Just me and my musings, if you please.

Harvesting Thoughts from the Abyss

In the depths of night, thoughts crop up,
Like weeds in my mind's busy cup.
Should I laugh or just corrupt?
Does sleeping count if I don't sup?

With a sock as my puppet on this head,
I negotiate reasons not to get out of bed.
"Today'll be fun!" my plush bear said,
While I snort at ideals I never bred.

The abyss whispers jokes, I snicker and sigh,
Who needs a sage when I'm this fly?
With each rolling laugh, I reach for the sky,
Harvesting musings as time slips by.

So deep in the night, let laughter burst,
Thoughts like confetti, oh, how they thirst.
In this mess of a mind, I've learned to trust,
That humor trumps worries and turns rust to dust.

The Mind's Haven

Upon this bed, a fortress strong,
Battling boredom, where I belong.
With pillows high, I sing my song,
As woes dissolve, and laughter throngs.

The clock ticks on, but I don't care,
Lost in a comedy, light as air.
Is the world mad, or is it rare?
Through giggles and thoughts, life's a fair.

With each weird notion I dare to shout,
My bed's a stage, I turn about.
In this haven, I twist and scout,
Finding joy in the silly rout.

So let the world spin with its stress,
In my sanctuary, I feel blessed.
With whims and laughs, I confess,
This cozy life is truly the best.

Resting Beneath the Weight of the World

I ponder life from my soft nest,
Why do socks vanish, is it a test?
The universe spins with comical grace,
As I search for reason in this warm space.

My pillow's wisdom I can't ignore,
Does it hold secrets of a cosmic store?
Dreams float around like jellybeans,
A reality check? Nah, just routines.

Goldfish swim in thoughts of the grand,
While I lie here, remote in hand.
Do the stars laugh at my sleepy quest?
Or do they simply think I'm the best?

Amidst my dreams, joy has a say,
Decisions are easier in the sleepway.
So here I rest, from the worldly grind,
With wit as my blanket, it's peace I find.

Serenity and the Search for Reason

In a rumpled quilt, I seek the truth,
Why can't cats be scholars, uncouth?
Are toasters really just time machines?
Or do they wish to serve bread with greens?

The clock ticks on, I sip my tea,
What if the meaning is just to be free?
With every tick, my thoughts take flight,
Chasing the essence of day and night.

Each ripple of sleep plays a prank,
As I plot my plans from my cozy tank.
Wouldn't it be grand if chairs could talk?
Perhaps they'd plot and floss, then walk!

Here in my haven, the world's quite chill,
I ponder snacks, and the thrill of the grill.
Nothing's too serious in this mental spree,
Except maybe that book… yeah, I'll read it at three.

The Universe Cradled in Cozy Corners

With every creak, the bed hums loud,
Are we just stardust lost in a cloud?
Between sheets, I wrestle with fate,
Plotting my next move on a pillow plate.

An alien peeks through the window light,
Wondering why I haven't taken flight.
Perhaps they too find Earth quite dull,
While I munch on chips, my mind in a lull.

Thinking if gravity is really that great,
Or just a scheme to keep us in straight?
Might as well float in this sweet dream state,
While knowledge must wait—what's on my plate?

So here I lay, with curious glee,
Contemplating life, like a bumblebee.
The universe spins in a cozy dance,
And I bumble about, waiting for my chance.

Introspection Underneath the Sheets

Wrapped in warmth, thoughts swirl like cream,
Who knew deep musings could start from a dream?
If socks have a party, do they invite shoes?
Or do they just laugh at our daily blues?

I'm a warrior fighting fluff in the night,
Battling the blankets till it feels right.
Do cucumbers ponder their salad fate?
Or just relish the veggies they celebrate?

Under these layers, the world seems absurd,
As I whisper my thoughts, unheard, but stirred.
What if tomorrow the sun forgot?
Would we dance in the darkness, or just lose the plot?

In this cocoon of a fluffy embrace,
I conjure up wisdom like a warm space.
With laughter and quirk wrapped up in a blend,
Introspection with humor, life's greatest friend.

A Tapestry Woven in Dreams

Upon this mattress, I ponder fast,
Fluffy clouds and worries, all amassed.
Do sock gnomes really steal my pair?
Or is it just life, playing unfair?

Pillow fights with thoughts, soft and spry,
Dancing in circles as I wonder why.
If cows can jump over the moon so bright,
Then surely I can take flight tonight!

The Imprints of Midnight Questions

What if my dreams pay my bills someday?
And wakeful hours just fade away?
Is the pillow a portal to another land?
Where I'm crowned the ruler, fleet and grand?

Peeking at shadows, the clock's hands tick,
Is sleep a rich man's charming trick?
Or do blanket forts serve a higher goal?
To inspire those dreams in a comfy shoal?

Soliloquy in Soft Light

In the morning glow, I wake with a grin,
Did I really snore like a wild bear kin?
The stars must've laughed when I took my stand,
With one foot in the dream, isn't life so grand?

As I stretch and yawn, do clouds feel the same?
Can they ponder their fluff as they float without shame?
With wisdom of teabags, steeped in a cup,
I just might find out if I ever get up!

Awakened Reflections

Scratching my head at these daily thoughts,
Is life just a game with mismatched socks?
When do we stop and just let it be?
While the cat on the bed eye-rolls at me!

Chasing my dreams like a sleepy owl,
Wondering if wisdom really has a vowel.
As I drift off again, don't let it end,
For tomorrow's adventures, my pillows will mend!

The Soft Symphony of Inner Voices

Whispers dance upon my ears,
In a chorus of my silly fears.
Pillows speak of dreams untold,
While blankets hug and keep me bold.

Sleepy thoughts take center stage,
Wrestling with my morning wage.
Daring optimism drips like rain,
As I giggle at my lonesome brain.

Cereal cravings creep and crawl,
Yet here I am, not moving at all.
What if the world spins without me?
Maybe I could just sip tea.

In this world of quilted muse,
No one cares if I snooze.
Each voice sings a different key,
And I nod along, just full of glee.

Navigating Life's Labyrinth from a Fuzzy Nest

Under quilted clouds I lay,
Charting maps, I drift away.
Socks are lost, but dreams are clear,
Existence feels like a game of beer.

Navigating through my thoughts,
Dodging all those tangled knots.
Should I rise or stay in place?
Life's a race, but this is grace.

A squirrel's tale becomes profound,
In my mind, wisdom is found.
Should I be wise or just make jokes?
The universe chuckles, shrugging folks.

Chaos reigns in cozy land,
Planning meals with a missing hand.
Why rush when I can ponder here?
A quest for snacks, my greatest fear!

Silent Dialogues in the Twilight Hour

Night approaches, silence steals,
While cotton dreams turn into feels.
Conversations within my head,
Bring laughter from my sleepy bed.

The moon becomes my sage tonight,
With stars that twinkle, oh so bright.
What if I'm a superhero here?
Just a pillow fight from conquering fear.

Thoughts collide like a traffic jam,
Should I be wise or just a sham?
Pretending to solve life's big schemes,
While plotting my escape with dreams.

In twilight's glow, my musings flow,
I giggle at the cosmic show.
A funny dance of light and dark,
All wrapped up, I find my spark.

Cosmos of Thought Beneath My Blanket

Starlit wonders hide from sight,
In my fortress made of white.
Galaxies swirl in cozy folds,
While wisdom waits as I behold.

Should I rise to seek the truth?
Or munch some snacks and squeal with youth?
Thoughts are just a pillow's game,
Finding joy in silly names.

Spirals of ideas twist and turn,
And from this comfort, I will learn.
Rainy weather inside my head,
Let's toast to tales that need to spread.

A universe wrapped in my embrace,
Where every thought finds its own space.
Underneath, a laughter bright,
As I conquer dreams in sleepy light.

Questions Hanging Like Nighttime Stars

Why do socks vanish in the wash?
Do they join a sock-age war?
Is time just a trick of the clock?
Or is it hiding behind the door?

Do cats have secret lives at night?
Plotting world domination, it seems.
If I could fly, would pizza taste light?
Or is it still just one of my dreams?

When did I last see the sun?
It must be hiding under the bed.
Did it run off with my favorite pun?
Or is it taking a nap instead?

Are pillows the softest truth we know?
Cozy whispers, dreams that tease.
Do they hold the secrets of the show?
Or is that just a breeze?

Foods for Thought Served on Fluffy Cushions

Is cereal a soup or just a snack?
('Froot Loops' on the nightstand, stacked.)
Do marshmallows laugh when they melt?
Or cry cause the hot chocolate's unstealth?

When I munch on chips, do they talk back?
Do they know of all my midnight cravings?
Does chocolate ice cream give me the knack?
Or is it just my taste buds misbehaving?

If I could eat wisdom, what would it be?
A slice of pie with a side of glee?
Would wisdom taste sharp, or perhaps sweet?
Or is it just leftovers from last week's feast?

Can thoughts be fast food for the mind?
Do junk ideas always leave you blind?
Is there a buffet of reasons to smile?
Or just another "hold that thought" for a while?

The Secret Life of a Bedbound Dreamer

Do pillows have secrets they whisper at night?
Or are they just fluff with a penchant for light?
If blankets could talk, what tales would they weave?
Of snuggles and rumbles, both hard to believe?

Does the mattress store dreams of its own?
What stories of wanderers have it known?
Do ghosts roam the sheets, or do they play dead?
Always lurking around in my sleepy bed?

If I roll over, do planets shift too?
Or do stars giggle at what I might do?
What if my blanket showed me the stars?
Wrapped in soft comfort, I'll travel so far!

Is the teddy I hug a guardian true?
Or a stuffed critter holding my shoe?
If dreams were a movie, would I win an award?
Or be stuck watching reruns, forever ignored?

Constellations of Ideas Above the Sheet

If ideas hang like stars, where do they go?
Do they twinkle in thoughts that I don't know?
Is the moon an egg, sunny-side up?
Or a giant light bulb spilling from a cup?

If I could eat dreams, would they fill me up?
Or just leave me hungry, stuck in a rut?
If time's a river, am I just a stone?
Rolling with worries I can't condone?

What's the weight of a thought drifting by?
Does it float like a feather, or drop from the sky?
In the bed's cozy depths, do ideas collide?
Creating a universe where giggles can hide?

In the pool of my thoughts, can I dive deep?
Or is it too shallow for a restful sleep?
If I count all my dreams, will they run away?
Or will they stay close, here to laugh and play?

Philosophers in Pajamas: A Solitary Assembly

In cozy robes, they gather round,
Ideas floating, no sense to be found.
With breakfast crumbs on wisdom's throne,
They ponder life while half asleep, prone.

Socks mismatched, their minds in a haze,
They chase the meaning of laundry days.
One claims socks are the essence of love,
While snoozing softly, they dream of.

A donut's hole, profound and deep,
Holds more answers than they dare to keep.
With giggles echoing through the night,
They toast to life with coffee's might.

So here they sit, in fluffy delight,
Philosophers lost in hilarity's light.
In pajama pants with wisdom's grace,
They'll find the truth in the next snack's embrace.

In the Realm of Night

Under the covers, thoughts take flight,
In the realm where dreams delight.
Minds do wander, free from the grind,
In shadows where the answers unwind.

What if a pillow could share its views?
Or laundry piles had deeply rooted clues?
Each creak of the floor a secret unsaid,
Whispering wisdom from dreams long fled.

The night is ripe with laughs and schemes,
Tickling fancies, enacting dreams.
As blanket fort guards ideas so bright,
A kingdom of giggles till morning's light.

Cereal philosophers, spoons in hand,
Conquer the universe, dreaming so grand.
In the realm of night, where nonsense reigns,
They find life's truths wrapped in silly chains.

Every Shadow Speaks

In the twilight, shadows begin to talk,
Whispering riddles as they stroll and walk.
A chair's shadow swears it's a wise old sage,
While a sock claims to be a poet on stage.

The lamp declares it's the brightest star,
Throwing light on thoughts from afar.
Each flickering flame holds a secret or two,
As shadows giggle, saying, 'Who are you?'

With every corner hiding a jest,
Even the clock thinks it knows best.
Ticking wisdom through hours that pass,
Mocking dreams in a playful sass.

So listen closely, don't close your eyes,
For every shadow in the night is wise.
With laughter and quirks, they teach us to feel,
That life's just a joke; who spins the wheel?

Gathering Echoes While Wrapped in Warmth

Gathered in blankets, snug and tight,
Echoes of laughter dance in the night.
Questions float like marshmallows sweet,
As socks do tango on cold bedroom feet.

What is the purpose of that extra spoon?
Is it for dessert or a soothing tune?
Pondering tea bags that steep away time,
They sip slowly, with giggles in rhyme.

Footnotes of life linger over their heads,
Each whimsy debated amidst sleepy spreads.
Warmth wraps around like a friendly embrace,
As thoughts untangle in soft, comfy space.

So here they settle, sharing their dreams,
In whimsy and warmth, nothing's as it seems.
Echoes delight in this whimsical trail,
Where together at night, they giggle and sail.

The Dreamscape's Unraveling Mysteries

As the moon peeks in with a cheeky grin,
Whispers of dreams start to softly begin.
Cereal boxes hold vast histories,
Tales of adventures in soggy mysteries.

Under the stars, the mind opens wide,
Exploring dimensions where teddy bears ride.
Logic takes a nap, crazy takes the lead,
In a world woven with giggles and speed.

What if the floor is a portal to space?
Or the couch is a throne in a warm, fuzzy place?
With every blink, a new plot unfolds,
In a realm where warmth turns dreams into gold.

So let's celebrate these dreams on the run,
Where slippers and whimsy make life more fun.
For in this tapestry woven with grace,
Everyone's a philosopher, in this silly race.

Shadows of Knowledge in the Quiet Dark

In shadows deep, I ponder fate,
What's the point of staying up late?
Ideas bounce like springs in air,
While dust bunnies gather without a care.

The blanket's warmth, my cozy shield,
Protects me from the truths revealed.
Socks on my feet, a wise disguise,
Why think too hard? Just close your eyes.

Thoughts drift by like clouds of sheep,
Are they profound or just plain deep?
In this cocoon, my mind's a whirl,
Maybe tomorrow, I'll save the world.

Yet here I lie, in comfy bliss,
Contemplating if I'll ever miss,
The meaning of life, or just my snack,
Perhaps there's wisdom in a midnight snack.

A Flickering Candle and the Nature of Being

A candle flickers, casting doubt,
What's life about? I'll just pout.
Shadows dance, as thoughts collide,
Is this the truth? Or just my pride?

With every drip, the wax drips slow,
What's one more worry? Just let it go.
This comfy bed, my fortress strong,
Maybe right now, I'll just hum a song.

Am I alive, or just a dream?
In this bed, nothing's as it seems.
So I'll ponder, with a sleepy grin,
Do socks need mates, or is it a sin?

The flicker fades, my eyelids weigh,
Tomorrow's musings can wait 'til day.
For now, I'll giggle at the night,
And let the stars decide what's right.

The Sanctuary of Sleep and Its Secrets

In my blanket fortress, dreams reign supreme,
What are they made of? Not quite a theme.
I whisper to pillows, my fellow friends,
As laughter is loud, but the silence blends.

With socks mismatched and hair a mess,
I contemplate life, oh what a stress!
The secrets of sleep hide well, I swear,
A mystery deep in my cushy chair.

What if I dreamt of pizza slices?
Or cupcakes sprinkled with sweet spices?
I grin at the thought, let's take a chance,
Perhaps there's wisdom in a midnight dance.

Yet dawn arrives with sleepy sighs,
As wisdom retreats with the sunrise.
So for now, I'll snuggle tight,
And let dreams carry me through the night.

Unraveled Threads of Curiosity

A tug at curiosity, what a delight,
Why do we sleep? Is it wrong or right?
A thread pulled loose, it unravels wide,
Do we dream of dragons, or just the tide?

Why's the clock ticking, is time just rude?
In my cozy bed, it sets the mood.
Is knowledge profound, or just a jest?
Maybe it's all just a comfy rest.

Each fleeting thought, a bubble burst,
Should I be wise, or simply cursed?
With crumbs of chips piled here and there,
Should deep thoughts bother my late-night lair?

As sleep creeps in, I have to ask,
Is curiosity just a silly mask?
For in this bed, as I lay awake,
I'm here for nonsense, make no mistake.

The Space Between Dreams and Reality

Lying here in cozy sheets,
My mind takes flight through funny feats.
What if cows could talk just fine?
Would they sip lattes and dine on wine?

Between the stars and my old sock,
I ponder why clocks choose to mock.
If fish had feet and ran with glee,
Would they finally get to be free?

Moments of Wonder in Comfort's Nest

In this nest of pillows high,
I wonder 'bout the reasons why.
Do ants have meetings, wear cute ties?
Do geese hold debates where logic flies?

Here I'm safe from daily strife,
What if my cat planned to take my life?
While munching cookies, I feel a spark,
Is my snack stash really a zoo in the dark?

Musings Sparked by the Moon's Glow

As moonlight dances on my wall,
I giggle at my shadow's call.
What if the moon was just a cheese?
Would mice float by with expert ease?

With each twinkle, I start to muse,
Are socks rebelling, hiding their shoes?
If laughter could echo through the night,
Would it chase away my fridge's fright?

When Darkness Whispers to the Mind

When silence falls, the thoughts invade,
What if shadows played a charade?
Do light bulbs feel the pressure rise?
While pondering life with wild surprise?

In night's embrace, what questions bloom?
Can dust bunnies enjoy a room?
Do beds gossip while we dream?
Maybe they're plotting a wild ice cream!

Bathed in Moonlit Meditations

In the night, I ponder my fate,
Do socks really match, or do they just wait?
My pillow agrees, it nods with a smile,
Philosophy's easier when lounging a while.

The stars up above seem to wink and tease,
Are they just lights, or do they hold keys?
Should I ask them questions or is that absurd?
They might just reply with a twinkling word.

I lean back and toss my thoughts to the sky,
What's the point of it all, oh my, oh my!
Is the cheese on my pizza a truth to pursue?
Or a sign that the universe wants me to chew?

With moonbeams as pillows, I drift into sleep,
In dreams, I hold meetings with cats who can speak.
They tell me of meaning in labels and tags,
As I roll with the punches that life often drags.

Starlit Queries at Daybreak

At dawn's early light, I stretch without care,
Is life just a game, or more of a dare?
The coffee brews slowly, a ritual divine,
Should I take it black, or would cream be just fine?

The curtains are drawn, revealing the sun,
Each ray is a question; oh, where should I run?
Do my shoes really know where they want me to go?
Or do they just sit, plotting mischief below?

As toast pops up, there's a vision so clear,
Is bread just a canvas for buttered veneer?
The plate spins around with its edible art,
What if the jam holds the key to the heart?

So I laugh at my thoughts with a mouthful of cheer,
Life's questions are funny when breakfast is near.
Each bite's a reflection on what it could mean,
And the world's such a fool when it's still half-asleep.

Beneath the Weight of Night

Under blankets snug, I muse and I dream,
Is life really a puzzle or just a bad meme?
With shadows as friends, I seek out the truth,
What's wisdom in napping, or chores of my youth?

The clock ticks away, does it care what I think?
Or is it just ticking while I pour my drink?
If time is a thief, then I'm a great bluff,
Stealing sweet moments, though maybe not enough.

With my lids growing heavy, I ponder the stars,
Are they just distant twinkles or natural scars?
If wishes are granted while sleeping in bliss,
Should I wish for more dreams or a bacon-ish kiss?

In the depth of my comfort, I wonder aloud,
Does life have a punchline, or am I too proud?
Each gasp of the night brings a chuckle or sigh,
As I wrestle with thoughts that refuse to die.

Soft Shadows of Inquiry

In the quiet of dusk, my mind starts to race,
Are dreams just the past dressed in a new face?
Each shadow a whisper, a hint of a jest,
What if my blanket holds secrets like zest?

The corners of night bring peculiar delight,
Should I kick off my covers and dance in the light?
Does the moon give a wink, or is it just me?
Trying to decode what the night wants to be.

If laughter is wisdom, it's hidden in snacks,
A bag of potato chips holds the world's missing facts.
When life seems too heavy, I'll make it a game,
To find all the giggles and never feel shame.

So I scribble my thoughts in the dark with a grin,
As I lounge in my haven, I embrace the din.
Let the shadows be guides to the quirks of my night,
For in humor, I find all the answers in sight.

Reveries on the Edge of Sleep

In the realm where dreams take flight,
I ponder if socks have feelings at night.
Do they long for a mate, or simply roam?
Perhaps they just wish to stay home.

A sandwich whispers secrets to a pear,
Does it envy the crispness of fresh air?
I giggle at fruit, in their silly stance,
Wishing I could join their juicy dance.

The pillows debate, should they fight or hug?
As I nestle in tight, just a little snug.
My blanket claims wisdom from times long past,
Yet all it really knows is the night's forecast.

Slumber's a play, I'm the star in the show,
Where the curtains are drawn, and the wild dreams flow.
Laughter and snores meld in a soft hum,
As I navigate thoughts from my sleepy kingdom.

Sleeping Under a Canopy of Questions

Under stars that wink with a playful jest,
I wonder where lost socks go to rest.
Do they gather and laugh, or form a parade?
What a sock would say if it weren't afraid.

Pillows conspire, making puns about dreams,
They giggle as I unravel my seams.
Is there a pillow fight in the moon's glow?
The laughter erupts, in a silent show.

Mice in pajamas rush past in the night,
Are they off to a dance, or a cheese-fueled flight?
The thoughts swirl in circles, a whimsical game,
Are they merry little critters or just so insane?

My bed cradles musings wrapped in soft glee,
With a wink from my nightstand—oh, what can it be?
A world full of quirks, yet I choose to stay,
In this riddle of sleep where all here is play.

The Quietude of Unraveled Knots

In this cocoon where my thoughts unwind,
I muse on how socks seem so hard to find.
Do they stage a coup for the laundry room?
Or is it just me, in my sleepy gloom?

The whispers of blankets start to debate,
Is it high time for my dreams to await?
Do they sparkle with mischief, just wanting a ride?
On a journey through realms where no thoughts divide.

Is there a ruler made only of cheese?
I giggle in bed, just trying to tease.
While my brain flips through channels, thoughts take a leap,
What a wild ride on this path of lost sleep!

With each crinkle and wrinkle, my spirit feels light,
In the circus of dreams, I stretch and take flight.
The starlit gymnastics of comedic delight,
As laughter cloaks shadows, all through the night.

Echoes of the Subconscious

As I lounge beneath thoughts' playful streams,
I hear echoes of laughter in the realm of dreams.
Do chairs ever ponder where they've been sat?
Or simply embrace their cushy habitat?

A cat on a mission to conquer the night,
Pretending to stalk every slumbering light.
Does it count every whisper of sleep's soft breath?
Or perhaps it's an agent, in training 'til death?

Naps are the puzzles we piece together,
Their mysteries bind us, no matter the weather.
Scribbles on paper come alive in my mind,
As I chase after giggles, so whimsically unkind.

With every unraveling notion I find,
I nestle in joy, unencumbered, unlined.
In a world full of nonsense, where dreams never end,
I chuckle bright-hearted, just me and my bed-friend.

Conversations with Quietude

Why is the pillow so soft and wise?
It hears all my dreams, it never replies.
I ponder the meaning of both cheese and sleep,
Wonders of life, which I just can't keep.

The blanket whispers secrets of warm delight,
Telling me tales that stretch through the night.
I laugh at my worries, they seem so absurd,
When shared with a mattress, they never get heard.

The clock ticks away, mocking my late night spree,
Counting each second as I sip herbal tea.
Here in this haven, my thoughts take their flight,
As I chart the universe, simply wrapped tight.

Oh, wisdom arrives in the silliest forms,
Like why do I dance when the fridge still warms?
So here I will stay, 'neath my covers I'd tread,
A philosopher born from my pillow instead.

Second Thoughts Beneath the Warmth of Covers

In the cocoon of my blanket, I lay so snug,
Contemplating life over a nice, warm mug.
Each sip is a journey of nonsense and dreams,
Where logic is lost in the soft, fluffy seams.

Did I leave the stove on, or was it just smoke?
As I dive into pondering the life of a bloke.
With each little thought, I recoil in delight,
Do socks have feelings when pressed into tight?

The shadows are dancing, they're silly and bright,
Whispering secrets of the creeping night.
Do pillows have dreams? I like to believe,
That they soar through the clouds when we are reprieved.

Tomorrow I'll conquer the world, or maybe just bake,
But tonight I'm content with my sweet, sleepy break.
Wrapped up in wonder, my worries in hibernation,
Here in my fortress, I embrace contemplation.

A Reverie on the Edge of Sleep

As I drift to the edge, the world's a big joke,
Like socks on a cat or a chair made of smoke.
Thoughts tumble like tumbleweeds, rolling around,
In the quiet abyss, what wisdom is found?

Do dreams need direction or just play on their own?
Can they take you to places where skills can be honed?
With a twist and a turn, I giggle and gleam,
Should I plan for tomorrow, or just follow the dream?

Fuzzy creatures visit with giggles and grins,
They ponder my life like it's filled up with sins.
Yet all that I contemplate in this whimsical zone,
Is whether that pizza is really my own.

Oh, the joys of the night and its playful embrace,
Where worries dissolve in this shadowy space.
I laugh at the questions my mind tends to seep,
Embracing the wonder as I slip into sleep.

Twilight Musings in the Quiet Chamber

In the twilight hour, my musings take flight,
With a wink and a nudge, they bloom in the night.
What's the deal with apples? Are they really divine?
Or just crisp little snacks at the end of the line?

The shadows conspire, looking sly as they creep,
Causing ruckus and giggles in the stillness of sleep.
Do chairs have opinions on who takes the score?
When I get up to snack, do they dream of more?

Of all my great thoughts, which ones can I keep?
While pondering pancakes that taste like sweet sheep.
The curtains are flirting with the moon up above,
As I ponder the meaning of flowers and love.

Here in the chamber, where wisdom's absurd,
I trade all my worries for one foolish word.
Each chuckle and giggle, my nighttime delight,
As I muse in the dark, till the dawn brings in light.

In the Quietude of Slumber's Hold

Beneath the sheets, ideas fly,
As fuzzy dreams drift lazily by.
Should I conquer the world today?
Or just sleep a bit more and play?

The socks I lost have formed a team,
Plotting world domination in a dream.
As my pillow whispers sweet secrets,
I'm the ruler of fluffy regrets!

With every yawn, I ponder life,
Should I make cookies or start a strife?
Sleepy wisdom fills the air,
Though all I want is a cookie to share.

So let me think in this cozy nook,
While Netflix rolls, oh what a hook!
Tomorrow's worries can take their time,
For now, I'll nap and have my rhyme.

Musings in the Cocoon of Night

Under stars, I lie awake,
Contemplating every mistake.
If I could talk to my younger self,
I'd tell him, 'Don't put dreams on a shelf!'

Should I rise early or snooze and dream?
The clock's ticking, what does it mean?
Pajamas snug, the world awaits,
But here I stay, debating fates.

My cat judges my nightly quests,
Snoozing away without any rests.
In this chaos of thoughts untamed,
Is this wisdom, or just sleep claimed?

Each wrinkle in my sheets is profound,
An endless cycle of thought unbound.
Tomorrow might bring adventure grand,
But first, let me nap, forever planned!

Echoes of Tomorrow from a Dusk Nest

In this nest of pillows and dreams,
I ponder life and all its schemes.
Will I be a hero when sun meets sky?
Or keep avoiding it with a good pie?

What if wisdom's just pizza and sleep?
That's knowledge I'd gladly keep.
Midnight snacks, a feast for thoughts,
Proving to my tummy, they are not fraught!

With each giggle of the moon's bright face,
I wonder if I'm in the right place.
Do socks have feelings? Is that a thing?
In bed, I'm a poet who can't help but sing!

The world outside waits with bated breath,
While I'm pondering life, and avoiding death.
So here I lie with jokes at the ready,
In Dusk's sweet arms, my mind is steady!

The Portrait of Thought in Pajamas

Attired in threads of swirling fun,
Pondering if I truly need to run.
Thoughts in plaid, wearing a grin,
Why chase the day? Let the day begin!

Is breakfast an idea, or just nice fluff?
With syrupy dreams, never enough.
My pillow's a canvas for all my fears,
Yet it holds them softly, easing my tears.

In these jammies of bright color flair,
I muse on life, and my wild hair.
What if I painted the stars tonight?
But only if I can keep it light!

From under my blanket, laughter does bloom,
Creating a gallery of thoughts in my room.
So here's to dreams with a wink and a nudge,
In the portrait of pajamas, I joyfully trudge!

www.ingramcontent.com/pod-product-compliance
Lightning Source LLC
Chambersburg PA
CBHW071850160426
43209CB00003B/488